Asset Allocation
The key to
Financial Security

Samuel Blankson

ISBN: 1-4116-4091-8

ACKNOWLEDGEMENTS

I give all thanks to God for filling my cup abundantly. Special thanks to my wonderful wife Uju, for curbing my greed and always reminding me to apply asset allocation.

CONTENTS

INTRODUCTION

Asset allocation is the key factor that will determine the duration and in some cases the probability for success in your financial freedom. Without a proper asset allocation in place, your investments are constantly at the risk of being wiped out by an unpredictable financial or economic disaster.

Divorce settlements, lawsuits, business failures, stock market crashes, bank failures, fraudsters, natural disasters, terminal illness, or death, are all potential life events, against which you have to protect yourself and your family. Using asset allocation will help you on the finance front of this battle for security.

A proper asset allocation plan will progressively improve your security, whilst you securely building you wealth. It will give you a secure playing field to grow your financial freedom. No single event will be able to affect your entire portfolio negatively, and in most cases, because of diversification, your portfolio may benefit from such a disaster.

We will look at what asset allocation is, how to plan and implement your own, and how to maintain and grow your assets within the framework of your new asset allocation.

Samuel Blankson

CHAPTER 1

What is Asset Allocation

What Is Asset Allocation?

Asset allocation is the process of allocating funds to different asset classes. This system and tool is used by fund managers and portfolio managers. Determining your asset allocation is more important than actually trading, as a wrong asset allocation will erode your returns, no matter how great the underlying assets in your portfolio are.

Many people including some portfolio managers and professional fund managers forget to apply asset allocation to their private and personal investments. They trade their personal portfolios with ego and emotion, thinking that disasters only happen to others.

Are you like that? Perhaps you have a great savings scheme with your bank, where you have placed all your funds. Remember BCCI. On the other hand, perhaps you have all your funds in your home. Remember the high interest rates of the 80's or the natural disasters that exhausted insurance companies, leaving many homeowners insolvent.

Do not make the mistake, as many before you have, in thinking you are immune to these disasters. They happen to all of us. Take active steps to protect yourself from them by diversifying your assets and allocating your investment funds across different asset, and risk classes.

Benefits Of Applying Asset Allocation To Your Investment Portfolio?

Applying asset allocation principles to your investment portfolio will not only decrease the effects of disasters, but it will help you take advantage of the inherent opportunities hidden within disasters.

For instance, during a market crash, if you applied asset allocation to your investments, you would have the vast majority of your investments in secure assets that would be untouched by the market crash. Therefore, when others are wiped out, and equity and property prices are at an all time low, you can use some of your secure investments to snap up these bargains, thus reaping great profits when the market later recovers.

This is the purpose and benefit of a good asset allocated portfolio, to build your wealth. If you do not begin with this, you could end up having to start over again because some unexpected disaster like the March 2000 stock market crash occurred. Take heed to this wise advice. Start by allocating assets to the four categories: Security, Buy and Hold, Momentum, and Lifestyle.

Lifestyle should be the last category you spend your money in, as financially, it is a hole in the ground. Cars, designer clothes, holidays, electronic gadgets etc, will not return any interest. In some cases as with cars and private jets, they will actually cost you money to keep them. In addition to this, aim to use returns from investments to increase your lifestyle, not your salary, or your main income source(s).

Investment Categories

The proper allocation of investment funds to assets can be achieved by taking your age and current financial position into consideration. Therefore, let us get started and learn about each investment category, and how much you should allocate to it.

The four investment categories that we will now cover are as follows:

1. Security
2. Buy and Hold
3. Momentum
4. Lifestyle

Security

Security products protect you against a negative downside.[1] Examples of these are a will, life insurance, critical illness insurance, health plan, pension plan, and tax-exempt savings instruments.

Buy And Hold

These are assets with tax-exemption or without tax-exemption, and with the potential for a negative downside. These products do not qualify for the Security category. Examples of these are real estate, precious metals (gold, silver platinum etc), precious stones (ruby sapphire diamonds etc), shares, fine wine, funds, and bonds, etc. These products generally have a maximum loss potential of your initial investment plus sales commissions. At the worst case, you will only loose what you put into them (unless you used margin to buy them).

Momentum

Momentum consists of assets with a high risk factor, offering potentially high positive upside returns, as well as potentially high negative downside losses i.e. options, futures, and spread betting etc. These products may have an unlimited loss potential as you could loose more than you originally invested in them.

Momentum products achieve their high potential swings due to gearing. Gearing is the use of a small amount of funds to control a larger amount. For instance, you could purchase a futures contract with $1,000 of your real money. This $1,000 could however, be geared to control $100,000. Thus, a 10%

---

[1] Financial instruments grow in value, or decrease in value. When they have the potential to grow in value, we say that they have a positive upside. When they have the potential to decrease in value, we say that they have a negative downside.

swing in your favour would earn you $110,000, of which you would keep $10,000 in profits. On the other hand, a 10% swing against you would have you loose $10,000 of your own real money.

Lifestyle

Strictly speaking, Lifestyle is not an investment category. It is included here because you will learn how you can make lifestyle spending that will enhance your wealth. Lifestyle investments maintain, or elevate your lifestyle, social status, or personal pleasure. Investment into antiquities, art, and collectables such as (cars, planes, boats, real estate, baseball cards, fashion items, and other collectable memorabilia) can grow in value with time. Therefore, you can enjoy them now, and later get back your money, including profits, when you want to sell them.

Structure For Security

Learn from the Egyptian pyramids. They have lasted for thousands of years because they were designed with a strong base and made to last the test of time. Make sure that your foundation for financial freedom is made up of Security products and investments. Figure 1 illustrates the ideal secure and sturdy structure formed when this balance is implemented through correct asset allocation.

As you can see, the pyramid is secure, resting on a base of security. Once this secure base is established, you can build the next level on top, Buy and Hold. Finally, you complete your asset allocation with a small allocation into Momentum products. Any surplus funds from your investments can then go towards your Lifestyle spending.

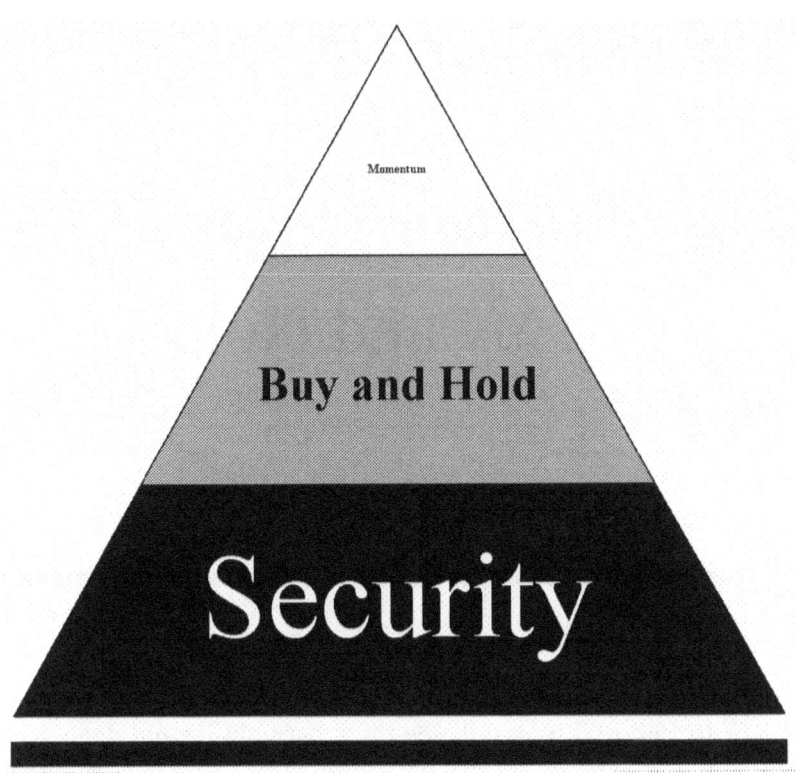

Figure 1: Ideal balanced asset allocation (N.B. Momentum is represented by the white triangle above Buy and Hold)

In Figure 2, you can see that you will have a weak base if you invest more in Buy and Hold, and less in Security. This structure will not stand for long. It only takes a stock market crash, or economic downturn, and your whole investment structure would topple.

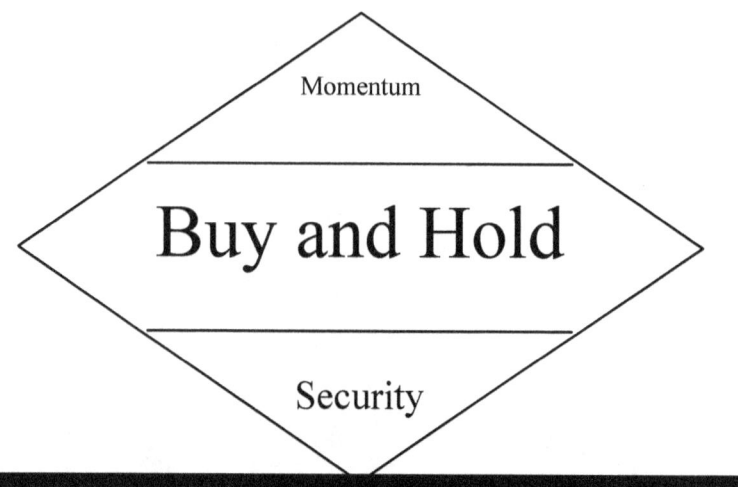

Figure 2: Over-investment in Buy and Hold

In Figure 3, you will see the most volatile and dangerous structure you could build. By having most of your investments in Momentum products, with few of your assets in Security, you stand a chance of being completely wiped out by the slightest unexpected turn in the markets.

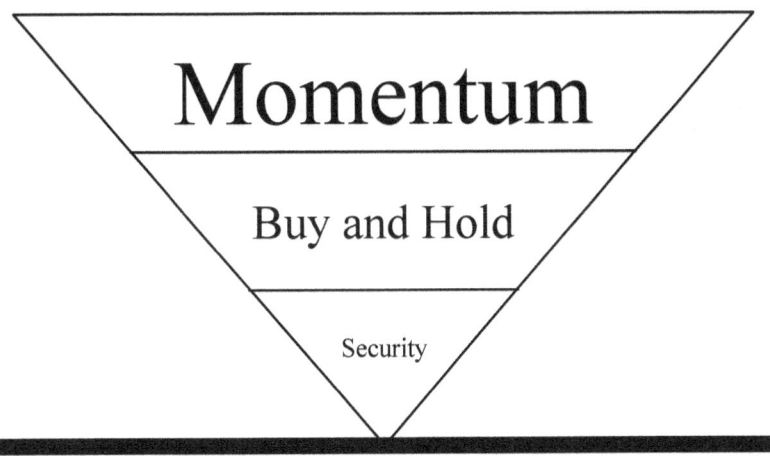

Figure 3: Over-investment into Momentum

The structure you select will greatly affect your future security, therefore, you should choose carefully. You will look next at how you can determine your tailor made asset allocation strategy and apply it.

CHAPTER 2

Determining Your Asset Allocation

Determining Your Asset Allocation

Defining your asset allocation requires you to take two things into consideration, your age, and your current financial situation. You only need these two criteria because; your age will determine your potential earning time span. This is how long you can earn a good income, and your current financial situation will determine how you should begin.

Considerations

Age

As you grow older, your ability to earn income decreases. This is because of three reasons. Firstly, you will slowly loose the use of your faculties, and therefore you will be growing physically and mentally unable to do the same tasks as younger more able-bodied people can. Secondly, you may face ageism with employers and clients, progressively forcing you out of the employment and business market. Thirdly, you may choose or be forced into retirement by your employer.

Because of these three reasons, you need to build security and take less financial risks nearing your retirement age. Your asset allocation strategy should represent and cater for this by increasing your Security allocation, as you grow older.

Current Financial Situation

Your current financial situation will also determine how the distribution of funds occurs. Generally the poorer you are the less financial risks you should expose to yourself, whilst the wealthier you are the more you can afford to dabble in risky investments.

In the case of the wealthy investor, if the investment goes sour and you end up loosing your invested funds, you will be able to recover, whilst if a poor person looses their funds in a risky investment, it could mean not being able to eat for the week, or filing for bankruptcy.

You should aim to invest most of your assets and investment income into Security products and investments that are free from a negative downside. In addition to this, you should aim for all investments in the Security category to be exempt from tax. We will now look at the two key considerations for determining how you apply asset allocation. These two factors are age and your current financial state.

Age

Below 30

If you are at below 30 (in the group furthest away from retirement age), you may want to increase your Buy and Hold and Momentum allocations to lean more on the riskier side, as you have the time to recover from potential disasters to your Buy and Hold and Momentum assets. However, you must maintain a minimum of 40% allocation to security products and investments.

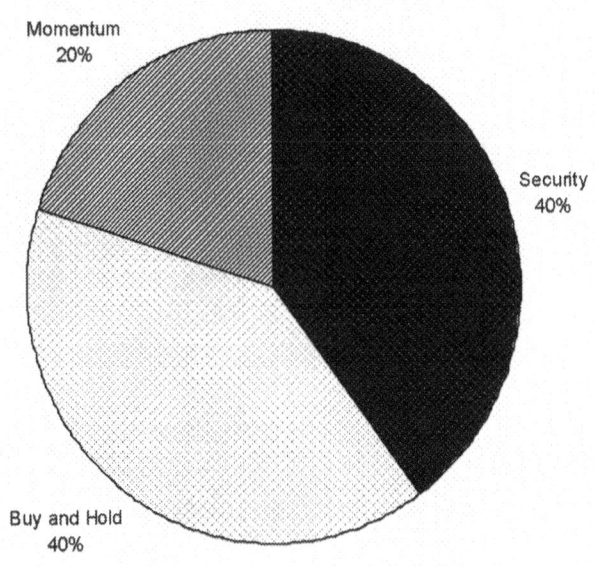

Figure 4: Furthest from retirement age - asset allocation (below 30)

30 To 50

Those in the middle-aged group of 30 to 50 should consider a more middle ground asset allocation style. Neither too risky nor too security focused.

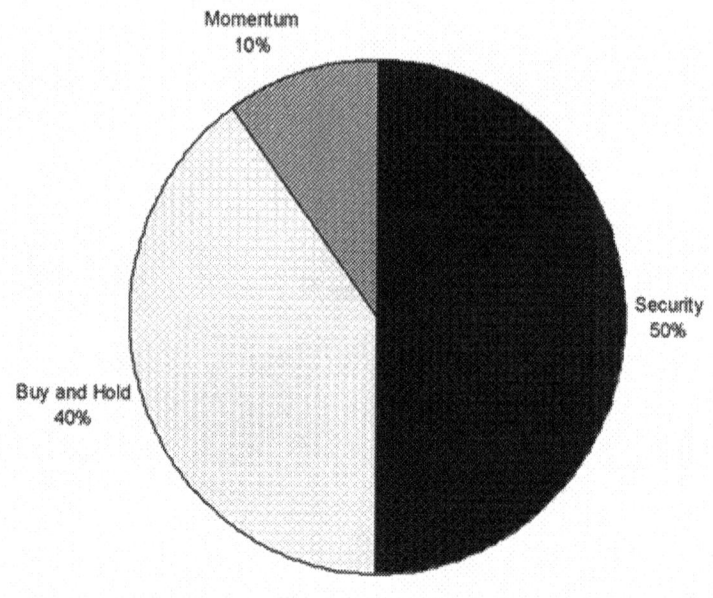

Figure 5: Middle-aged - asset allocation (30 to 50)

50 Plus

Those of you who are 50 plus, and therefore close to retirement age, should increase your Security allocations and decrease your riskier assets.

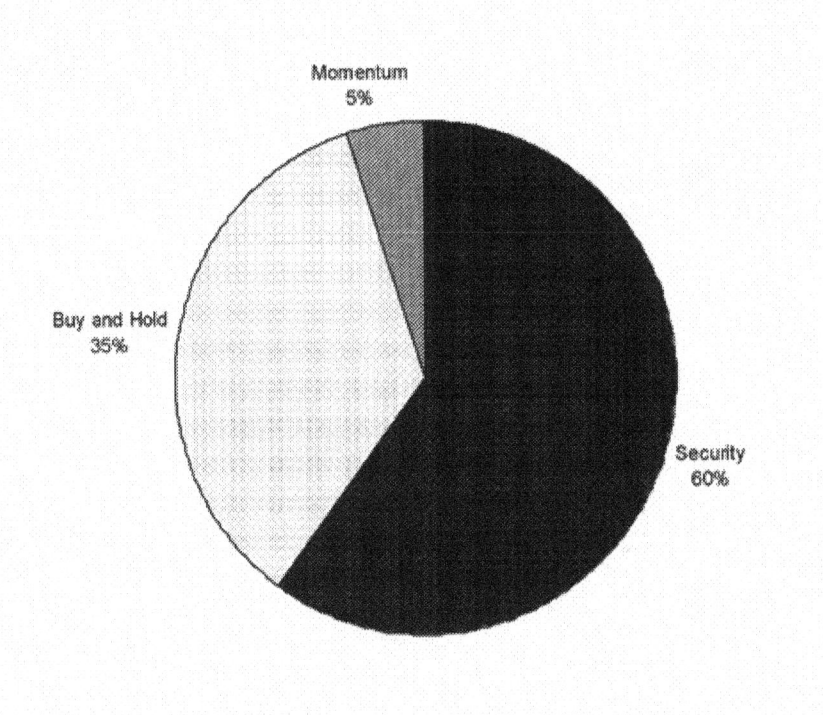

Figure 6: Near retirement age - asset allocation (50 plus)

I mentioned earlier that there were two considerations. You have looked at the first one, age. Now let us look at the second, your current financial state.

Your Current Financial State

We will break this section into three groups: the poor, the well off, and the rich.

The Poor

These people should not invest in anything but Security products and investments, as they cannot afford any downside risk. It does not matter how much money you earn, if you spend more than you are making then you should only invest into Security products and investments (if you have any disposable income available).

Note: If you are in this category, you can get out of it by reading and applying the advice in the book, *How to Destroy Your Debts*. Until you are no longer in this category, you should not invest in any Buy and Hold or Momentum products, or investments.

The Well Off

The second group, the well off, are those who spend less than they make and have no debt, except perhaps a mortgage. If you are in this group, you will have disposable income and thus can afford to invest into Buy and Hold investments. If you are in this group, apply the asset allocation of Figure 4. Until you are free from all debt, which includes your mortgage, you should not invest into any Momentum products or investments.

Note: Incidentally, reading and applying *How to Destroy Your Debts* would also help those in this category, especially in clearing your mortgage in a fraction of the time it would normally take.

The Rich

Those who have no debt and spend less than they make, will be able to use the age considerations previously covered, to decide how to allocate their assets.

Therefore, you can afford a little risk if you have no debts and are living within your means. A maximum of 20% of your assets (although 5%-10% is recommended), and investment income can be allocated to assets in the Momentum[2] class. Make

---

[2] Figure 4, Figure 5 and Figure 6 are based on the maximum allocations.

sure however, that you do not lower your Security class allocation below 40%, no matter what your situation.

Your Aspirations

You may aspire to great wealth, and thus you believe that you must increase your allocation into the Buy and Hold and Momentum group. Great and high aspirations are good; however, do not pursue them with foolishness. Decreasing your Security group allocation below 40% is nothing short of foolishness. This foolishness is often inspired by greed.

Contrary to Gordon Gekko's belief, greed is not good. If you are contemplating placing yourself in the wrong category, i.e. the Rich category, when you currently belong in another category, i.e. the poor category, you will only be delaying the time it takes to become financially free. You could also be decreasing your security, and inviting disaster to befall you.

Do not invest more into the Momentum group thinking that you will catch up with your Security assets when you have made a fortune. You will only worsen matters, or worse still, you could end up bankrupt. If you do not want to apply the advice in this book on Asset Allocation, please do not invest or acquire assets, as you will only do yourself harm.

To get ahead faster, work harder, and decrease your lifestyle spending. By cutting back on luxury purchases, you will have more to distribute, according to your asset allocation plan, towards the Security, Buy and Hold, and Momentum group products and assets. Aspire to great wealth, but stick to your asset allocation plan, and you will achieve it.

CHAPTER 3

Applying Your Asset Allocation

Applying Your Asset Allocation

Having a strategy is only of use if you apply it. This is true of your asset allocation strategy. You will now know what percentages you need to apply to each investment group. Now you need to assign your current investments into these groups, and determine their investment fund allocation.

Acquire four lined pieces of paper and at the top of each, write one of the four investment groups, "Security", "Buy and Hold", "Momentum", and "Lifestyle".

Security Definition

The definition of Security products and assets is as follows:

"Investments or insurance products that are inherently designed to only experience an upside".

This means that the value (baring inflation), of the asset can only increase.

If you have any of the following products or similar products and investments, list them on the Security sheet. (Note that your pension plan is a buy and hold product as it can rise or fall in value).

- All insurances (Medical [Life, Critical Illness, Long Term Care, Dental Care, Health Plan etc], Home, Car Insurance, Travel etc)
- Will
- Fixed Income Government Bonds (US, Canadian, Western European countries, Switzerland, Japanese, Australian, etc)

Government bonds are included in this list with a warning. Make sure the government is stable and able to fulfil the bond agreement within the life of the bond. Some governments are unstable, and thus, a bond in such a government might as well be a lottery ticket. Consult *"The practical Guide to Total Financial Freedom: Volume 2"* for more information on bond trading.

Buy And Hold Definition

The definition of Buy and Hold products and assets is as follows:

"Investments or securities products that are inherently designed to facilitate upside and downside price movement".

This means that the value (baring inflation), of the asset can rise as well as fall, but you are unlikely to loose more than you invested.

If you have any of the following products or similar products and investments, list them on the Buy and Hold sheet.

- Bonds
- Stocks and shares
- Pension plans
- Funds (Mutual Funds, Hedge Funds etc)
- Property/real-estate
- Precious metals and stones (gold, Silver, Diamonds etc)
- Life policies (Viaticals etc)
- Wine
- Collectables (memorabilia, baseball cards, antique furniture and motor vehicles etc)
- Art

Momentum Definition

The definition of Momentum products and assets is as follows:

"Investments or securities products that are inherently designed to facilitate the use of gearing. Therefore they can experience great highs and potentially great lows".

This means that the value (baring inflation), of the asset can rise greatly as well as fall disastrously. With this asset class, it is possible to loose more than you initially invested.

If you have any of the following products or similar products, and investments, list them on your Momentum sheet.

- Spread betting
- Gambling
- Options and futures
- Businesses
- Race horses

With any of the above products and investments, a bad decision could cost you your initial investment as well as your home and potentially more.

Lifestyle Products Definition

The definition of Lifestyle products is as follows:

"Investments or purchases, made primarily for entertainment or enjoyment. These products normally depreciate in value with time and are not good investments at all."

This means that the value (baring inflation), of the asset will normally only fall. With this asset class, it is possible to loose more than you initially invested.

For instance, if you buy a sports car, you will need to insure it fuel it repair it as well as pay road tax, and possibly other annual taxes. In the lifetime of the vehicle, you could spend more in upkeep, taxes, and insurances, than you initially paid for the car. At the same time, the vehicle will be depreciating in value at a rapid pace, in some cases by 15% or more a year.

If you have any of the following products or similar products and investments, list them on your Lifestyle sheet.

- Designer clothing
- Designer shoes
- Designer accessories
- Jewellery
- Motor vehicles
- Airplanes
- Boats
- Holiday Homes
- "Bad habits" (alcohol, hard drugs, Cuban cigars etc)

The only reason Lifestyle is covered in this book is that, with careful planning and shopping, you can turn some Lifestyle products into collectible investments that appreciate in value with time. Normally any product that is rare and in high demand, or that will come to be in high demand sometime in the future, is a good candidate as a Lifestyle investment.

There are two things to watch out for with Lifestyle investments, these are as follows:

1. Always insure them.
2. Avoid high financial maintenance products like jet planes, boats, and motor cars. These will eat away all future appreciations in the assets value.

Most of the time Lifestyle purchases will have bad investments returns. This is because by their very nature they were not meant to be great investments. In this case, all you can do is to thoroughly, enjoy them.

Allocation Distribution Within The Asset Classes

Now that you have assigned all your assets to their correct asset classes (Security, Momentum, Buy and Hold, and Lifestyle), let us discuss how you determine how much to assign to the individual assets within the class. For this exercise, there are two rules. These are as follows:

1. Do not over diversify
2. Do not under diversify

Over Diversification

This begs the question "how do you know when you are over diversified?"

The answer to that question is not simple. To find the answer to this question you need to understand why you need to diversify in the first place.

Diversification is the process of spreading your investment risk. For instance if you buy equities and bonds, you are covering both possibilities of the market movement. When the stock values fall, investors generally move their assets into bonds or cash. Therefore, investing in bonds will prove to be less risky during these periods. Generally, on the other hand, when equity values rise, investors abandon bonds, and move into stocks and shares.

This movement also correlates to interest rate changes. High interest rates generally mean better returns on fixed income bonds, as they pay out on a fixed interest rate, whilst low interest rates are great for stocks and shares. This is because during low interest rates, companies can borrow more money at a lower cost, and thus, they can purchase more raw materials and invest in growth. This investment, if successful, will improve profits for shareholders by raising the share price of the company.

Security Diversification

So back to over diversification, the only asset class you cannot over diversify in is the Security class. This is because in this class, there is very little risk of loss, as all the qualifying investment products in this class do not normally experience a downside. (I say normally because, if for instance, another World War broke out, no investment class will be totally secure).

Buy And Hold Diversification

The Buy and Hold class requires more thought and planning before distributing your investment funds. Property, funds, bonds, stocks and shares, wine, and gold are a few of the products in this class. Some of these products have a higher risk factor. For instance, gold is normally less risky than funds, and funds are normally less risky than stocks and shares.

This is a general rule because there are some high-risk funds that invest in Momentum products like futures and options. These Hedge funds will always be more risky than normal stocks and shares. This type of fund belongs in your Momentum class of assets.

When investing in any asset type like stocks and shares, bonds property, gold etc, aim to diversify your investments across five or more products. For instance, if you are investing in Gold, diversify by investing in five or more gold products:

- Gold Bullion Bars & Coins
- Canadian Maple Leaf
- Australian Kangaroo
- Chinese Panda
- Austrian Philharmonic
- English Britannia
- American Eagle
- South African Kruggerand
- English Britannia

- Mexican Centenario Family
- Gold Statement Accounts
- Gold Accumulation Plans
- Gold Mining Shares
- Gold And Silver Index
- Gold Mutual Funds

Please note that the Gold and Silver index, gold mining shares, and gold mutual funds belong to the gold asset type, as well as also belonging to other investment types (i.e. stocks and shares and funds).

Similarly, when investing in stocks and shares, invest across, at least, five stocks, in at least five different sectors: You can choose from the following selection of sectors:

- Aerospace and Defense
- Automotive
- Banking
- Chemicals
- Computer Hardware
- Computer Software
- Conglomerates
- Construction
- Consumer Durables
- Consumer Non-Durables
- Diversified Services
- Drugs
- Electronics
- Energy
- Financial Services
- Food and Beverages
- Health Services
- Insurance
- Internet
- Leisure
- Manufacturing

- Media
- Metals and Mining
- Real Estate
- Retail
- Specialty Retail
- Telecommunications
- Tobacco
- Transportation
- Utilities
- Wholesale

Choose different sectors to invest in, to avoid bad news in a particular sector adversely affecting your portfolio. In an ideal world, you would diversify across different markets too. This however, is difficult for the personal investor to achieve with stocks and shares. Funds can achieve this type of diversification. For more on stocks and shares, consult *How to Make a Fortune on the Stock Markets, ISBN: 1411623797.*

There are many funds, covering global, sector, industry, economy, market, and indices. Diversifying through funds requires you selecting funds that invest in different areas, i.e. US, Europe, Asia, Emerging markets or a whole selection of others. Consult *Making Money With Funds, ISBN: 1411626710.* When investing in funds, select at least five, and spread the risk.

In the case of real estate, you can choose to diversify through location and type of real estate investment. It is not a good idea to invest all your real estate allocation into one property, in one area. If you are just starting, out and do not have the funds to diversify with your real estate investments, do not invest in real estate. Wait until you can start with at least five real estate investments before adding real estate to your portfolio.

Choose geographically separated real estate and select different types of real estate investments to invest. Consult *The Guide to Real Estate Investing, ISBN: 1411623835.* The following is a listing of the different types of real estate investments:

- Subletting rental real estate
- Renting real estate to do business from
- Buying commercial real estate to let
- Buying commercial real estate to do business from
- Buying a home to live in - an asset that appreciates.
- Buying residential real estate to let
- Investing in multi-family real estate
- Developing real estate
- Using off-plan
- Real estate deal using WRAPs
- Quick sale or flipping real estate
- Buying and selling foreclosed real estate
- Investing in Real Estate Investment Trusts (REITs)
- Investing in real estate mutual funds
- Investing in real estate limited partnerships.
- Investing in high yield private mortgage notes.
- Invest in education to become a real estate professional.

Be aware that the risk levels involved in all these real estate investment types vary, and each investment project has to be considered on an individual basis.

Momentum Diversification

Concerning the Momentum asset class products like options, futures, high yield investment programs, and spread betting etc, apply the same principles discussed for Buy and Hold. Always diversify using Calls and Puts or Write contracts to lock in options premiums, etc. Consult *How to Make a Fortune with Options Trading, ISBN: 1411623789.*

Lifestyle Diversification

To say you are diversifying into the Lifestyle class is perhaps humourous. Any investment into this class should be made from returns made from investing in the other classes Buy and Hold and Momentum), and not from the Security class, your employment or business income. This will be difficult to do at first, but once you start living this way, you will find it a secure and relaxing way to enjoy your money. It will automatically force you to live within your means and avoid keeping up with the "Joneses".

Another way to schedule the acquisition of lifestyle products, is to set an investmnet goal. Once you achieve this goal, you can go out and purchase the Lifestyle class product as a reward. Consult *Planning and Goal Setting, ISBN: 1411637747,* for further information on delaying gratification and setting goals to achieve financial success.

Asset Class And Asset Type Diversification

If you find that your portfolio only contains one type of asset from the Buy and Hold, Momentum or Lifestyle group, you are under diversifying in that asset group, and over diversifying in that asset type.

For example if you only have stocks and shares in your portfolio, you need to diversify and invest in some funds, bonds, real estate, precious metals etc. Otherwise, when the next stock market crash comes along, your portfolio may be wiped out.

Building Wealth Through Redistribution

The key is to keep money in your Security class products until you can allocate the funds into five or more assets in an asset type within the Buy and Hold class.

To summarise, over diversification only exists with Buy and Hold, Momentum, and Lifestyle products. Security class products have a guaranteed return and thus you cannot over diversify in them. There will be no profit dilution when you invest in many Security class products.

However, in the Buy and Hold, Momentum and Lifestyle class products, you can over diversify. This happens when you invest in, contradicting, asset types that negate the gains and losses, of your portfolio. In effect causing your portfolio to not appreciate, or depreciate.

To get around this, always make sure you are invested in assets that are growing in value, diversify into many assets types in each asset class and take profits regularly from your assets and redistribute according to your asset allocation plan into all asset classes.

For example, if you make 10% gains in your Buy and Hold asset class portfolio, on stock you own. After selling the stock, take the 10% and assign 50% of it to Security, 40% to Buy and Hold, and 10% to Momentum (if that is your asset allocation distribution plan).

With every gain you make, redistribute the profits according to your asset allocation into the different asset classes. Therefore, if your asset allocation were 50% to the Security class, 40% to the Buy and Hold class, and 10% to the Momentum class, then you would allocate all profits you make accordingly.

By applying this redistribution with every gain you make, you will secure a large percentage of all your gains and risk less of your profits. Over time, this strategy will yield you a fortune, affording you a secure financial future.

Summary To Asset Allocation

You have read the importance of allocating your assets and investment income according to your age and financial situation. To be successful in investing, and to build financial freedom, you will need to read and reread this book, then apply the advice.

If you loose, squander or erode your earned income again, and again, this cycle will only stop when you start to apply the Asset Allocation principle to your investments. To secure and guarantee your financial success, apply Asset Allocation to your assets and investments, then when a disaster comes along, you will be better protected against it.

Come back to this book whenever you go off course. Asset Allocation is the most important subject to consider when planning your personal financial freedom. By learning to assign the correct proportions of your investment and income to Security, Buy and Hold and Momentum products and investments, you will build wealth and be able to use the surplus interest to invest in improving and enjoying your life.

NOTES

Asset Allocation

OTHER WORKS BY SAMUEL BLANKSON

How to Destroy Your Debts

Printed: 165 pages, 6.0 x 9.0 in, Perfect-bound
Download: PDF (1739 kb)
ISBN: 1-4116-2374-6
Copyright Year: © 2005 by Samuel Blankson
Language: English
Publisher: Lulu.com

If you are like me, you hate being in debt! Every month you watch, your money run out before the end of the month. You scrape around for fuel and grocery money, and then finally you hit the credit cards, hoping they hold sufficient funds.

If you want to get out of this cycle of worry over debt, this book may be your answer. I say, "May," because although this book will definitely give you techniques for controlling, managing, and even getting out of debt altogether, it will not do the work for you. That will be up to you.

This book will reveal how to destroy your debts, including your mortgage. It will also make clear to you how you can increase your income, and have confidence in your financial future. Your journey to financial freedom begins here.

The Practical Guide to Total Financial Freedom: Volume 1

Printed: 124 pages, 8.5 x 11.0 in, Perfect-bound
Download: PDF (7761 kb)
ISBN: 1-4116-2058-5
Copyright Year: © 2005 by Samuel Blankson
Language: English
Publisher: Lulu.com

The first part of a five volume series on creating Total Financial Freedom. In this volume, you will learn the foundations of wealth building, and how to secure your family and your wealth against disasters and losses.

This series offers practical, effective, and easy to follow advice for securely and quickly building wealth. If you are thinking of buying this book, you probably want to be free. Free from the rat race, free from the boss, free from the wage trap, and free from the mediocrity and hopelessness of poverty and lack of options. Until now, you may have had no other way of achieving this within the next half a decade.

This book will change all that forever. This book, unlike many self-help books out there, will actually tell you what to do in order to achieve Total Financial Freedom. You will find out exactly how I went about achieving Total Financial Freedom. If you read, learn, and apply the lessons in this book, you too will achieve Total Financial Freedom.

The Practical Guide to Total Financial Freedom: Volume 2

Printed: 173 pages, 8.5 x 11.0 in, Perfect-bound
Download: PDF (31040 kb)
ISBN: 1-4116-2057-7
Copyright Year: © 2005 by Samuel Blankson
Language: English
Publisher: Lulu.com

The second part of a five volume series on creating Total Financial Freedom. In this volume, you will learn how to invest in Bonds, Stocks and Shares, and Funds.

This series offers practical, effective, and easy to follow advice for securely and quickly building wealth. If you are thinking of buying this book, you probably want to be free. Free from the rat race, free from the boss, free from the wage trap, and free from the mediocrity and hopelessness of poverty and lack of options. Until now, you may have had no other way of achieving this within the next half a decade.

This book will change all that forever. This book, unlike many self-help books out there, will actually tell you what to do in order to achieve Total Financial Freedom. You will find out exactly how I went about achieving Total Financial Freedom. If you read, learn, and apply the lessons in this book, you too will achieve Total Financial Freedom.

The Practical Guide to Total Financial Freedom: Volume 3

Printed: 143 pages, 8.5 x 11.0 in, Perfect-bound
Download: PDF (1716 kb)
ISBN: 1-4116-2056-9
Copyright Year: © 2005 by Samuel Blankson
Language: English
Publisher: Lulu.com

The third part of a five volume series on creating Total Financial Freedom. In this volume, you will learn how to invest in En Primeur Wine, Real Estate, Businesses, Life Insurances, Art, and Offshore investment opportunities.

This series offers practical, effective, and easy to follow advice for securely and quickly building wealth. If you are thinking of buying this book, you probably want to be free. Free from the rat race, free from the boss, free from the wage trap, and free from the mediocrity and hopelessness of poverty and lack of options. Until now, you may have had no other way of achieving this within the next half a decade.

This book will change all that forever. This book, unlike many self-help books out there, will actually tell you what to do in order to achieve Total Financial Freedom. You will find out exactly how I went about achieving Total Financial Freedom. If you read, learn, and apply the lessons in this book, you too will achieve Total Financial Freedom.

The Practical Guide to Total Financial Freedom: Volume 4

Printed: 134 pages, 8.5 x 11.0 in, Perfect-bound
Download: PDF (3961 kb)
ISBN: 1-4116-2055-0
Copyright Year: © 2005 by Samuel Blankson
Language: English
Publisher: Lulu.com

The fourth part of a five volume series on creating Total Financial Freedom. In this volume, you will learn how to trade and invest in Momentum products. These instruments are high-risk products that offer high returns, but also the possibilities of high losses.

You will learn how to limit those losses by reducing the risk using effective and practical methods. Options, Futures, High Yield Investment Programs, and Gambling are some of the exciting topics covered in detail. This series offers practical, effective, and easy to follow advice for securely and quickly building wealth.

This book, unlike many self-help books out there, will actually tell you what to do in order to achieve Total Financial Freedom. You will find out exactly how I went about achieving Total Financial Freedom. If you read, learn, and apply the lessons in this book, you too will achieve Total Financial Freedom.

The Practical Guide to Total Financial Freedom: Volume 5

Printed: 322 pages, 8.5 x 11.0 in, Perfect-bound
Download: PDF (7143 kb)
ISBN: 1-4116-2054-2
Copyright Year: © 2005 by Samuel Blankson
Language: English
Publisher: Lulu.com

The last part of a five volume series on creating Total Financial Freedom. In this volume, you will learn how to lower your taxes, avoid paying unfair and unnecessary taxes, and how to move offshore and pay no taxes at all.

This series offers practical, effective, and easy to follow advice for securely and quickly building wealth. If you are thinking of buying this book, you probably want to be free. Free from the rat race, free from the boss, free from the wage trap, and free from the mediocrity and hopelessness of poverty and lack of options. Until now, you may have had no other way of achieving this within the next half a decade.

This book will change all that forever. This book, unlike many self-help books out there, will actually tell you what to do in order to achieve Total Financial Freedom. You will find out exactly how I went about achieving Total Financial Freedom. If you read, learn, and apply the lessons in this book, you too will achieve Total Financial Freedom.

Living the Ultimate Truth, 2nd Edition

Printed: 166 pages, 6.0 x 9.0 in, Perfect-bound
Download: PDF (855 kb)
ISBN: 1-4116-2375-4
Copyright Year: © 2005 by Samuel Blankson
Language: English
Publisher: Lulu.com

Today most people live a poor example of a balanced life. The centuries of wisdom passed down from the great leaders of our past seem lost amid lives centred on minutia and selfishness.

Today we care more about what we wear and where we are seen, than we do about discovering and Living the Ultimate Truth. Throughout the world, there is an imbalance in people's spirituality, consciousness, and inner harmony. This has taken a great toll on our environment, our health, and our happiness. Many are wondering around like lost sheep, seeking a shepherd in all the wrong places.

Many false prophets have promised quick fixes to these problems, but if these solutions are not firmly rooted in The Creator, love, integrity and inner harmony, they are doomed to fail.

This book is a reminder of all those virtues and universal principles that we need, to return to a balanced, harmonious, and happy life. You will learn to love yourself, love others, and finally find that inner peace you seek through spiritual growth.

Developing Personal Integrity, 2nd Edition

Printed: 118 pages, 6.0 x 9.0 in, Perfect-bound
Download: PDF (627 kb)
ISBN: 1-4116-2376-2
Copyright Year: © 2005 by Samuel Blankson
Language: English
Publisher: Lulu.com

In the field of human character development, integrity is the last frontier. Many people use the word, but few really know what real integrity is.

This book breaks down the fundamental components of personal integrity and offers a path to attaining it. Like success or happiness, integrity is a journey not a destination.

We can only measure how far on the path we are through the observation of our inner voice, the voice of our conscience, and through deep contemplation and reflection.

This journey of personal excellence is not an easy one, and as a friend once said, "When peeling this onion, sometimes you cry." Nevertheless, in all great endeavours, the harder the struggle, the greater the victory will be.

The Guide to Real Estate Investing

Printed: 117 pages, 6.0 x 9.0 in, Perfect-bound
Download: PDF (723 kb)
ISBN: 1-4116-2383-5
Copyright Year: © 2005 by Samuel Blankson
Language: English
Publisher: Lulu.com

If you have ever wanted to know how to make money from real estate, but could never find one source that listed and explained all the different options available to you, then your search is over.

This book covers over 20 different ways of investing in real estate. You will find the author's style easy to understand and very practical. The section on self-build is so in-depth, that after reading it you will actually know how to build a house, and the section on REITs, Indexes, and REIT Options will leave your mind boggling at the potential profits available to you.

This book also covers the conversional and popular methods of real estate investing as well. Therefore, whether you want to learn to develop real estate projects, build your own home, or simply rent a room in your house, this book will help you maximise your success and avoid the pitfalls.

Tax Avoidance A practical guide for UK Residents

Printed: 104 pages, 6.0 x 9.0 in, Perfect-bound
Download: PDF (355 kb)
ISBN: 1-4116-2380-0
Copyright Year: © 2005 by Samuel Blankson
Language: English
Publisher: Lulu.com

UK residents pay some of the highest taxes in the world. Most of these taxes are hidden through VAT and service charges. This guide clearly explains what taxes you are paying, and which ones you can and should avoid paying through claiming your allowed deductions and allowances. Prudent tax efficient estate planning is explained in detail, and hundreds of tax saving ideas are shared within these pages. Whether you are a qualified accountant or a non-professional, you will find this little guide an invaluable source of tax saving ideas and strategies.

Making Money with Funds

Printed: 79 pages, 6.0 x 9.0 in., Perfect-bound
Download: PDF (8769 kb)
ISBN: 1-4116-2671-0
Copyright Year: © 2005 by Samuel Blankson
Language: English
Publisher: Lulu.com

Today the world fund market is a multi trillion-dollar industry. There are many types of funds and as many reasons for choosing them. In this book, you will learn how Funds work, and how you, can make money with them.

How to make a fortune with Options trading

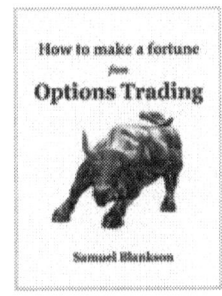

Printed: 59 pages, 8.5 x 11.0 in, Perfect-bound
Download: PDF (1808 kb)
ISBN: 1-4116-2378-9
Copyright Year: © 2005 by Samuel Blankson
Language: English
Publisher: Lulu.com

This is a practical book on winning in the Options trading market. Whether you are a sophisticated investor or a complete novice, this book is for you. The author takes complex ideas, and explains them in a way that is both practical and easily understood by anyone. Having used these techniques to achieve financial freedom, Mr Blankson now shares with you how he did it. There is no waffling here, just plain speaking and powerful techniques that anyone can apply.

How to make a fortune on the Stock Markets

Printed: 190 pages, 8.5 x 11.0 in, Perfect-bound
Download: PDF (8769 kb)
ISBN: 1-4116-2379-7
Copyright Year: © 2005 by Samuel Blankson
Language: English
Publisher: Lulu.com

This book contains simple but effective techniques for achieving regular and consistent profits from stock trading. Unlike other books on the topic, it is not full of theory and projections, but practical advice learned the hard way, by trading personal hard-earned cash daily in the world's stock exchanges. Moreover, unlike other books on the subject, it is not about how to be a stock trader and trade other people's money, but on how to grow your own funds to a level where you will never have to work for anyone else again.

This book contains real techniques used by the author to amass a fortune significant enough to have made him Financially Free. Now you too can use these simple but highly effective techniques to achieve the same results. Therefore, whether you are a professional trader or a total beginner, this book will show you how to achieve Financial Freedom through trading Stocks and Shares.

Attitude

Printed: 418 pages, 6.0 x 9.0 in, Perfect-bound
Download: PDF (13700 kb)
ISBN: 1-4116-2382-7
Copyright Year: © 2005 by Samuel Blankson
Language: English
Publisher: Lulu.com

Attitude, so often misunderstood, yet so vital for success in every aspect of our lives. A positive attitude will guarantee happiness in your life, promotion, and growth in your career or job, peace and joy in your family life, and in addition, a positive attitude has been scientifically proven to help extend your life expectancy. In this book, this essential success attribute is explained in detail. You will learn how to safeguard against positive attitude erosion, and learn how to build a positive mental attitude to help you achieve measurable success in every aspect of your life.

How to Win at Online Roulette

Printed: 81 pages, 6.0 x 9.0 in, Perfect-bound
ISBN: 1-4116-2570-6
Copyright Year: © 2005 by Samuel Blankson
Language: English
Publisher: Lulu.com

This is a guide to consistently winning at online Roulette. It is a simple and to the point writing about an amazing system for gaining an advantage at online Casinos. This book will show you how to make £1000 per day or more from online Roulette.

The Ultimate Guide to Offshore Tax Havens

Printed: 418 pages, 8.5 x 11.0 in, Perfect-bound
Download: PDF (12602 kb)
ISBN: 1-4116-2384-3
Copyright Year: © 2005 by Samuel Blankson
Language: English
Publisher: Lulu.com

This book is a detailed listing of all the known and not so commonly known Tax Havens, their benefits, and their suitability for relocation by the low tax seeker. If you are looking for ways to cut your taxes, there is no better way than to relocate to a low or no tax haven. The South East Asian Tsunamis and earthquakes have shown us that it is prudent to select the haven you will reside in carefully. Low taxes cannot be your only gauge for this task. This book will help you make that decision.

A must read for all who aspire to changing their lifestyles by relocating offshore. The havens are listed in geographical order, starting with the USA and ending with the South Pacific Islands.

How to win at Greyhound betting

Printed: 68 pages, 8.5 x 11.0 in, Perfect-bound
Download: PDF (639 kb)
ISBN: 1-4116-2377-0
Copyright Year: © 2005 by Samuel Blankson
Language: English
Publisher: Lulu.com

Today, sports betting is a big industry for the bookmakers and organisers. Of all the people who benefit from sports racing, the "punters" (or in this case, you), are the last on the list of people who consistently gain. In fact, the greyhounds probably gain more from these races than most punters. Why is that? Well, there are many reasons, but most of them centre on these two things: lack of a proven system, and greed. This book closely examines these two points, and offers techniques and systems for achieving consistent wins in greyhound betting.

Images of Kilimanjaro

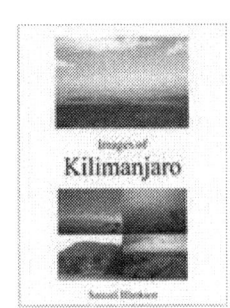

Printed: 53 pages, 8.5 x 11.0 in, Perfect-bound
Download: PDF (2573 kb)
ISBN: 1-4116-2016-X
Copyright Year: © 2004
Language: English
Publisher: Lulu.com

This is a book of pictures taken from Kilimanjaro. This is an accompanying book to the Calendar of the same name.

The Ultimate Greyhound Betting System

Download: MS Excel (233 kb)
Copyright Year: © 2005 by Samuel
Blankson
Language: English
Publisher: Lulu.com

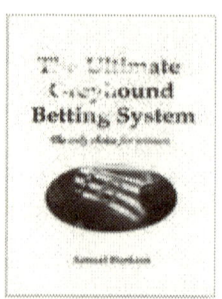

If you think there is no trustworthy betting system out there, then prepare to be proven wrong. This is the betting system described in the series *The Practical Guide to Total Financial Freedom,* and the book *How to win at Greyhound betting.* This semi-automatic system allows its user to achieve a minimum of 30% profits per week by following a proven statistical and rule based system betting on UK Greyhound races. The system only requires you to supply the race results and place the bets with your bookmaker. Armed with this incredible system, you will be able to beat the odds, and win one over the bookmakers.

Sixty Original Song Lyrics

Printed: 200 pages, 6.0 x 9.0 in, Perfect-bound
Download: PDF (1072 kb)
ISBN: 1-4116-2059-3
Copyright Year: © 2004 by Samuel
Blankson
Language: English
Publisher: Lulu.com

This is a compilation of original song lyrics by Samuel Blankson. This book contains 60 of the songs he wrote in between 2000 – 2002. Having had some of these lyrics made into songs for an album (see *www.practicalbooks.org*), and several of them now on compilations, Samuel now shares these 60 song lyrics with you.

Images of Kilimanjaro

Printed: 26 pages, 11 x 8.5 in, Coil-bound
Start Date: January 1st, 2006
Duration: 12 months
Copyright Year: © 2004 by Samuel Blankson
Language: English
Publisher: Lulu.com

Kilimanjaro, the tallest freestanding mountain in the world, is captured here for you to feast your eyes on each month through 2006. Kilimanjaro is a source of life for Tanzania and Kenya locals, who live on its life giving rains and water. I had the honour of climbing this majestic mountain, and captured the essence of its allure and mystery through these pictures.

Uju

Download: MPG (6523 kb)
UPC: 4-3157-3526-2
Copyright Year: © 2004 by Samuel and Uju Blankson
Language: English
Publisher: Lulu.com

A six track EP with soulful R&B tracks with a pop flavour. This EP is bound to have you humming along addictively. For more info about the artist Uju, visit *www.uju-music.com* and look out for her forthcoming album.

The Bass by Samuel Blankson

Download: MPG (4811 kb)
Copyright Year: © 2004 by Samuel and
Uju Blankson
Language: English
Publisher: Lulu.com

A sexy, R&B track with wicked beats and a deep baseline. With a melody and chorus that will stay with you for a long time, this addictive and catchy tune deserves your download (see *www.practicalbooks.org*).

Investing in En Primeur Wine

Printed: 88 pages, 6.0 x 9.0 in, Perfect-bound
Download: PDF (1,095 kb)
ISBN: 1-4116-2867-5
Copyright Year: © 2005
Language: English
Publisher: Lulu.com

Wine investing is not new, it has been going on for centuries. In more recent years (the last two centuries), government tax laws on alcoholic drinks have made buying wine a little more prohibitive to the investor who wants to keep them at home in his/her private cellar. Nevertheless, as usual, the market has found a way around this problem.

You can avoid taxes and V.A.T. (Value Added Tax) by buying fine wine on Bond (also called wine Futures or En Primeur). This book covers a simple and effective way in which anybody coming into the fine wine investing market place can safely securely and successfully select, and invest in En Primeur Wine.

Eight Steps to Success

Printed: 105 pages, 6.0 x 9.0 in, Perfect-bound
Download: PDF (1,095 kb)
ISBN: 1-4116-2738-5
Copyright Year: © 2005
Language: English
Publisher: Lulu.com

We would all like to live a successful life, a life where our relationships and finances are a source of happiness and joy. This life is attainable by following timeless success principles. These principles have been forgotten by our fast food, fast-paced, reality TV society.

This book defines, explains, and shows you how to apply these principles and skills in your life to attain happiness, contentment, peace, joy, and prosperity. The eight fundamental virtues and skills required to succeed long-term in any endeavour, are explained in detail and in a style that everyone can understand and immediately apply.

The Eight Steps to Success is an inspirational book that will help you understand, acquire, hone, and apply the principles of success.

Taking Action

Printed: 105 pages, 6.0 x 9.0 in, Perfect-bound
Download: PDF (1,095 kb)
ISBN: 1-4116-2735-0
Copyright Year: © 2005
Language: English
Publisher: Lulu.com

This is a book about taking action. For some, taking action means something you will do, might do, should do, have done, or never will do. This book will show you how to change your understanding of taking action to mean something you are doing NOW! When you change this focus in your life, you will release great powers. This book will show you how to tap into this phenomenal power and change your life.

Paris 2006

Printed: 73 pages, 8.5 x 11.0 in., Coil-bound
Download: PDF (12103 kb)
ISBN: 1-4116-3691-0
Copyright Year: © 2005
Language: English
Publisher: Lulu.com

Romance, love, chic, fine dining, all these can be found in abundance in Paris, the city of lights. Through the pictures in this enchanting book, you will always be reminded of the charm and beauty of Paris.

Images of Kilimanjaro In Colour

Printed: 73 pages, 8.5 x 11.0 in., Coil-bound
Download: PDF (4093 kb)
ISBN: 1-4116-3680-5
Copyright Year: © 2005
Language: English
Publisher: Lulu.com

When you are climbing Kilimanjaro, you will get very familiar with "Pole Pole". The Phrase uttered by your guide means "slowly slowly" in Ki-Swahili. As you look at these beautiful pictures of Africa's tallest mountain, that phrase comes to mind. You just cannot help but take it slowly for the rest of the day. This mountain has that sort of effect on you, and these pictures have captured this tranquil majestic beauty for you to savour all through the year.

The Heart of Moscow (Calendar)

Printed: 26 pages, 11 x 8.5 in., Coil-bound
Copyright Year: © 2005
Language: English
Publisher: Lulu.com

The heart of Moscow is captured here in these glorious pictures. Each picture shows a different side of this mysterious and historically rich city. Now you can enjoy the heart of Moscow with each passing month through 2006.

The Heart of Moscow

Printed: 73 pages, 8.5 x 11.0 in., Coil-bound
Download: PDF (8417 kb)
ISBN: 1-4116-3684-8
Copyright Year: © 2005
Language: English
Publisher: Lulu.com

The heart of Moscow is captured here in these glorious pictures. Each picture shows a different side of this mysterious and historically rich city. However, far from showing you the sites of Moscow, these pictures have captured the mysterious essence that is Moscow today.

Paris 2006 Calendar

Printed: 26 pages, 11 x 8.5 in., Coil-bound
Copyright Year: © 2005
Language: English
Publisher: Lulu.com

Romance, love, chic, fine dining, all these can be found in abundance in Paris, the city of lights. Through the enchanting pictures in this calendar, you will be reminded of the charm and beauty of Paris all through 2006.

Planning and Goal Setting For Personal Success

Printed: 200 pages, 6.0 x 9.0 in., Perfect-bound
Download: PDF (12103 kb)
ISBN: 1-4116-3774-7
Copyright Year: © 2005
Language: English
Publisher: Lulu.com

This book is about planning and goal setting to achieve success in the eight areas of your life. These areas are as follows:

1. Spiritual
2. Family
3. Relationships
4. Community
5. Charity
6. Educational
7. Financial and career
8. Recreational and fun

By learning to develop your dreams into achievable objectives with a time limit and associated reward for its achievement, you will create goals. Acting on your goals will bring success into your life. Working in all eight areas of your personal life will give you balance, harmony, and happiness. If you have not read this fantastic book, your life is loosing out on successes you deserve.

ABOUT THE AUTHOR

An entrepreneur at heart, Samuel Blankson blends art, creativity, passion, business acumen, and financial expertise with careful planning and execution in the achievement of measurable results. He is an avid reader, writer, researcher, and securities trader.

He is an advocate of self-empowerment and an individual's ability to control their destiny through the achievement of personal freedom from economic, financial, spiritual, social, mental, and interrelationship restrictions. Samuel is constantly working to push the boundaries of personal achievements to their limits, recognising that these limits are only self-imposed.

Samuel has authored over twenty books (*How to Destroy Your Debts*, *Living the Ultimate Truth*, *Developing Personal Integrity*, *The Practical Guide to Total Financial Freedom* volumes 1, 2, 3, 4 and 5, and *Attitude* are some of these works). He has written over 100 songs, sixty of which are featured in *Sixty Original Song Lyrics*. He writes poetry, creates artwork, and works daily to express his creativity in many ways.

Having successfully run several businesses, Samuel diversified into securities trading over a decade ago, with great success. After learning from the masters of the time, Samuel progressed to develop his own methods and systems for successful trading. Today, he trades many financial instruments and has developed ways of successfully generating profits from his many investments.

A firm believer in knowledge sharing, Samuel travels the globe, teaching and sharing his personal knowledge with groups of friends, associates, and anyone who seeks to improve their life. This is the spirit of Samuel Blankson, a God centred philanthropist, overcomer, and high achiever.